1-2-3
ZooBorns!

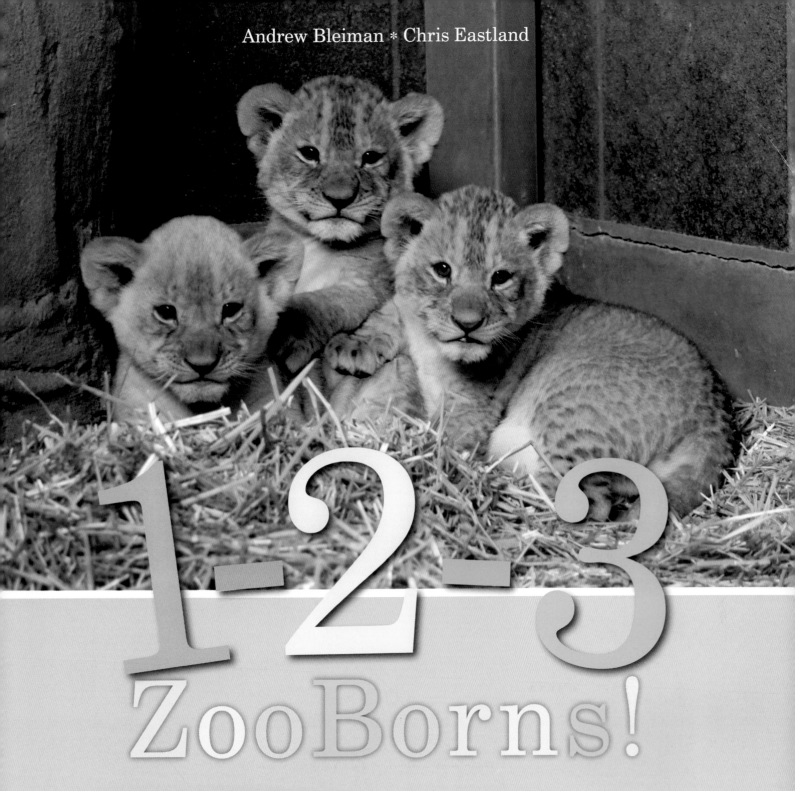

Andrew Bleiman * Chris Eastland

1-2-3
ZooBorns!

BEACH LANE BOOKS * New York * London * Toronto * Sydney * New Delhi

To my adorable niece, Maddy—A. B.

To my #1 pal, Georgie—C. E.

Special thanks to the photographers and institutions that made *1-2-3 ZooBorns!* possible:

Anteater: Saint Louis Zoo

Asian small-clawed otters (half-title page): Newquay Zoo

Black rhino: Vera Gorissen/Zoo Krefeld

Bobcats: Darlene Stack/Assiniboine Park Zoo

Capybaras: Twycross Zoo

Cheetahs (cover): Theo Kruse/Royal Burgers' Zoo

Cheetahs (hiding): Zoo Basel

Crane: Chester Zoo

Elephant: Tibor Jäger/Zoological Center Tel Aviv Ramat Gan Safari

Fishers: Minnesota Zoo

Giraffes: Shallon McReaddie

Guinea hogs: Shannon Calvert taken at Connecticut's Beardsley Zoo

Indian rhino: Zoo Basel

Jackals: Eva Bruns/NaturZoo Rheine

Koalas (embracing): Ellen Wilson/Taronga Zoo

Koalas (peeking): Taronga Zoo

Langurs: Paul Chamberlin/San Francisco Zoo

Lemurs: Longleat Safari & Adventure Park

Lion (eating): Ron Magill/Zoo Miami

Lions (title page): Omaha's Henry Doorly Zoo and Aquarium

Lions (racing and greeting): Jeffrey F. Bill/Maryland Zoo

Nigerian dwarf goats: Shannon Calvert taken at Connecticut's Beardsley Zoo

Ocelot: Sheri Hemrick/Cameron Park Zoo

Orangutan: Joseph Becker/Phoenix Zoo

Peccary (back cover): Sandi Wong/San Francisco Zoo

Penguin: Thom Benson/Tennessee Aquarium

Polar bear: Archive Zoo am Meer

Porcupine: Amiee Stubbs/amieestubbs.com

Pudu: Chester Zoo

Pygmy hippopotamus: Zoo Basel

Red pandas: Kristin McCoun/Lincoln Children's Zoo

River otter: North Carolina Aquarium at Pine Knoll Shores

Seal: Monika Kownacka/Wroclaw Zoo

Sloth: Sarah Woodruff/Zoo New England

Tamanduas: Staten Island Zoo

Tapir (racing): Dublin Zoo

Tapir (eating): Chester Zoo

Tigers: Jill Burbank taken at Indianapolis Zoo

Warty pig: Chester Zoo

Wombat: Paul Fahy/Taronga Zoo

OCLC 6-19-18

BEACH LANE BOOKS * An imprint of Simon & Schuster Children's Publishing Division * 1230 Avenue of the Americas, New York, New York 10020 * Copyright © 2015 by ZooBorns LLC * All rights reserved, including the right of reproduction in whole or in part in any form. * BEACH LANE BOOKS is a trademark of Simon & Schuster, Inc. * For information about special discounts for bulk purchases, please contact Simon & Schuster Special Sales at 1-866-506-1949 or business@simonandschuster.com. * The Simon & Schuster Speakers Bureau can bring authors to your live event. For more information or to book an event, contact the Simon & Schuster Speakers Bureau at 1-866-248-3049 or visit our website at www.simonspeakers.com. * Also available in a Beach Lane Books hardcover edition * Book design by Lauren Rille * The text for this book was set in Century Schoolbook. * Manufactured in China * 0717 SCP * First Beach Lane Books paperback edition October 2017 * 10 9 8 7 6 5 4 3 2 1 * The Library of Congress has cataloged the hardcover edition as follows: * First Edition * Bleiman, Andrew. * 1-2-3 zooborns! / Andrew Bleiman and Chris Eastland.—First edition. * p. cm. * ISBN 978-1-4814-3103-3 (hardcover) * ISBN 978-1-4814-3104-0 (eBook) * 1. Counting—Juvenile literature. 2. Zoo animals—Infancy—Juvenile literature. I. Eastland, Chris. II. Title. * QA113.B545 2015 * 513.2'11—dc23 * 2014045854 * ISBN 978-1-4814-9174-7 (pbk)

The baby animals in this book

want to help you learn your 1-2-3s!

But that's not all . . . these cute and cuddly newborn zoo critters have another very important job. By allowing us to observe and study them, they help us learn how to protect their wild cousins who live in jungles, deserts, mountains, and oceans around the world.

The more you know about animals, the more you too can help protect them. So come on in and meet the ZooBorns. Then visit your local accredited zoo or aquarium to learn more!

Paul Boyle, Ph.D.

Senior Vice President, Conservation Research & Development and Policy
Association of Zoos and Aquariums

The Association of Zoos and Aquariums sets high standards to make sure all the animals at accredited zoos and aquariums get the very best care.

1

ZooBorn riding.

2

ZooBorns hiding.

3

ZooBorns embracing.

ZooBorns
racing.

ZooBorns walking.

6

ZooBorns talking.

7 ZooBorns greeting.

8

ZooBorns eating.

9

ZooBorns peeking.

10

ZooBorns sleeping.

Nigerian Dwarf Goat

Black Rhino

Pudu

So many ZooBorns!

Elephant

Giraffe

Lemurs

Tiger

Red Pandas

Pygmy Hippopotamus

Polar Bear

Giraffe

Langur

Capybaras

Fishers

Seal

Guinea Hogs

Tamandua

Lion

Crane

Koalas

Tapir

Lions

Koala

Bobcats

Tiger

Nigerian Dwarf Goat

Wombat

Cheetahs

River Otter

Penguin

Jackals

Lions

Orangutan

Porcupine

Can you count them all?

Tapir

Sloth

Warty Pig

Anteater

Indian Rhino

Langur

Ocelot

Get to know the ZooBorns!

Species: Anteater (Giant)
Home: Saint Louis Zoo
Conservation Status: Vulnerable

Giant anteaters are native to Central and South America. They use their long, sticky tongues to catch and eat insects. During the first year of life, giant anteaters will spend much of their time riding on their mothers' backs.

Species: Bobcat
Home: Assiniboine Park Zoo
Conservation Status: Least Concern
Despite ranging across the United States and Mexico, this shy and secretive feline is rarely seen. Weighing about 20 to 25 pounds, bobcats might be mistaken for large house cats if not for their short "bobbed" tails.

Species: Capybara
Home: Twycross Zoo
Conservation Status: Least Concern
Capybaras spend much of their life submerged in swamps, so their eyes and ears are high on their heads to keep a lookout for predators above the water. They are the largest rodents in the world, growing to 150 pounds or more!

Species: Cheetah
Home: Royal Burgers' Zoo and Zoo Basel
Conservation Status: Vulnerable
Native to Africa, the Middle East, and India, cheetahs are the world's fastest land animals, reaching speeds of 75 miles per hour! Unlike other big cats, cheetahs are poor climbers.

Species: Crane (Black-Crowned)
Home: Chester Zoo
Conservation Status: Vulnerable

These cranes live in the sub-Saharan savannas in Africa. They like grasslands, especially wet grasslands, and can nest in trees. Both parents participate in rearing the young, usually 2 to 3 chicks at a time.

Species: Elephant (Asian)
Home: Zoological Center Tel Aviv
          Ramat Gan Safari
Conservation Status: Endangered
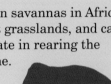
These elephants are native to Southeast Asia. They are smaller than African elephants and have smaller, rounded ears. Only males have tusks, unlike African elephants where both males and females have tusks. They love to fill their trunks with water and spray themselves.

Species: Fisher
Home: Minnesota Zoo
Conservation Status: Least Concern
Fishers are known for their tree-climbing, hunting, and agility. These solitary creatures are constantly on the move. In the wild, fishers raise their young in cozy dens beneath rocks, roots, or other found shelters.

Species: Giraffe
Home: Taronga Western Plains Zoo
Conservation Status: Least Concern, but the West African and Rothschild subspecies are Endangered

Giraffes live in the savannas, grasslands, and woodlands of Africa. They are the tallest land animals, and their necks are so long, they have to spread their front legs apart or kneel to take a drink.

Species: Guinea Hog
Home: Connecticut's Beardsley Zoo
Conservation Status: None (domestic)

This rare breed of swine originated in the United States. While once numerous in the Southeast, there are now only about 200. Guinea hogs are smaller than domestic pigs.

Species: Jackal (Golden)
Home: NaturZoo Rheine
Conservation Status: Least Concern
The golden jackal is native to parts of Africa, Europe, the Middle East, and Asia. It makes sounds similar to a domestic dog's and is omnivorous, eating fruit, vegetable matter, and meat.

Species: Koala
Home: Taronga Zoo
Conservation Status: Least Concern
Mother koalas carry their babies, called joeys, in their pouches until they are 6 or 7 months old. Koalas are native to Australia. They are arboreal, which means they live in trees.

Species: Langur (François')
Home: San Francisco Zoo
Conservation Status: Endangered
Baby François' langurs sport bright orange hair that turns black in adulthood. They live in large groups, and adults share parenting duties.

Species: Lemur (Ring-Tailed)
Home: Longleat Safari & Adventure Park
Conservation Status: Endangered
Ring-tailed lemurs often gather as a group to sunbathe in the morning. At night they split into sleeping parties and huddle together for warmth. Ring-tailed lemurs are found only on the island of Madagascar.

Species: Lion
Home: Omaha's Henry Doorly Zoo and Aquarium, Maryland Zoo, and Zoo Miami
Conservation Status: Vulnerable; the Asiatic subspecies is Endangered
The lion is the second largest cat, after the tiger. Lions live primarily in sub-Saharan Africa in social groups called prides that consist of related females and their offspring and a small number of adult males. Males have long hair around their necks called manes.

Species: Nigerian Dwarf Goat
Home: Connecticut's Beardsley Zoo
Conservation Status: None (domestic)
A miniature dairy goat originally from West Africa, the Nigerian dwarf goat is gentle and friendly and can be trained to walk on a leash. Its milk is high in butterfat, so it is often used to make cheese.

Species: Ocelot (Brazilian)
Home: Cameron Park Zoo
Conservation Status: Endangered
Found in Central and South America, this wildcat is sometimes called a dwarf leopard. It hunts rodents, lizards, frogs, birds, and fish at night and rests during the day, often in trees. Kittens stay with their mothers for up to 2 years.

Species: Orangutan (Bornean)
Home: Phoenix Zoo
Conservation Status: Endangered
Baby orangutans cling tightly to their mothers for the first 5 months of life. They remain with Mom for 7 years, one of the longest childhoods in the animal kingdom.

Species: Penguin (Gentoo)
Home: Tennessee Aquarium
Conservation Status: Near Threatened
Gentoo penguins are found in the Antarctic. The mother lays 2 eggs at a time, and both parents take turns incubating them for more than a month. They are very fast swimmers.

Species: Polar Bear
Home: Zoo am Meer Bremerhaven
Conservation Status: Vulnerable
The polar bear lives primarily within the Arctic Circle and prefers to hunt its favorite food, seals, from the edge of sea ice. After eating, a polar bear will wash itself with snow and water. Polar bears are excellent swimmers.

Species: Porcupine (Prehensile-Tailed)
Home: Nashville Zoo
Conservation Status: Least Concern
These porcupines live in the trees in tropical forests in Central and South America. Their tails are prehensile, which means they can use them to hold on to things. A baby is called a porcupette. Porcupette quills are soft at birth but harden in a week. If threatened, a porcupine may roll into a ball, protected by its sharp quills.

Species: Pudu (Southern)
Home: Chester Zoo
Conservation Status: Vulnerable
The pudu is the smallest deer in the world. The Southern species lives in the dense underbrush of the rain forests in Chile and Argentina. It escapes predators by sprinting and running in zigzags.

Species: Pygmy Hippopotamus
Home: Zoo Basel
Conservation Status: Endangered
Pygmy hippos are only half as tall as common hippos. They live in forests and swamps in West Africa, and they eat plants, grasses, and fruits, which they look for at night. During the day they stay in water to keep their skin cool and moist. They generally live in small groups or are solitary.

Species: Red Panda
Home: Lincoln Children's Zoo
Conservation Status: Vulnerable

Red pandas are native to the eastern Himalayas and southwestern China. They are about the size of a large domestic cat. Red pandas are born blind and develop very slowly. As adults, they are usually solitary. Despite their name, they are not closely related to giant pandas.

Species: Rhinoceros (Black)
Home: Zoo Krefeld
Conservation Status: Critically Endangered
Black rhinos have poor eyesight but good senses of smell and hearing—their ears can rotate in all directions. They are native to eastern and central Africa, and they are browsers, which means they eat leaves and twigs.

Species: Rhinoceros (Indian)
Home: Zoo Basel
Conservation Status: Vulnerable
Also called the greater one-horned rhinoceros, the Indian rhino's legs and shoulders are covered in wartlike bumps. It lives in grasslands and forests near riverbanks in India and Nepal, and it is a grazer, meaning it eats mostly grasses. Indian rhinos can run faster than 30 miles per hour and are excellent swimmers.

Species: River Otter (North American)
Home: North Carolina Aquarium at Pine Knoll Shores
Conservation Status: Least Concern
River otters are remarkably playful and love to wrestle and chase one another. They often slide down mud or snow into the water for amusement. Otters live in large, gregarious social groups of 15 or more individuals.

Species: Seal (South African Fur)
Home: Wroclaw Zoo
Conservation Status: Least Concern
These semiaquatic sea mammals often gather in colonies and live in the cold waters of the Southern Hemisphere. They spend their first few weeks of life on land and then begin to follow their mothers into the water for swimming lessons.

Species: Sloth (Linne's Two-Toed)
Home: Zoo New England's Franklin Park Zoo
Conservation Status: Least Concern

These large, furry mammals live in trees in South American tropical forests. They spend most of their lives dangling upside down from branches, and they sleep about 15 hours a day.

Species: Tamandua
Home: Staten Island Zoo
Conservation Status: Least Concern

Tamanduas are a type of anteater found in Central and South America. They use their 16-inch-long tongues to look for food like ants and termites, mostly at night. Instead of teeth they have a gizzard, an organ in the digestive tract used to grind up food.

Species: Tapir (Brazilian)
Home: Dublin Zoo and Chester Zoo
Conservation Status: Vulnerable

Brazilian tapirs live in tropical forests in Central and South America. They are born with spots and stripes to help camouflage them. They use their short trunks to grab leaves and fruit to eat. They are also excellent swimmers and will dive to feed on aquatic plants.

Species: Tiger (Amur/Siberian)
Home: Indianapolis Zoo
Conservation Status: Endangered

Amur or Siberian tigers are the largest living cats. Most of the 400 to 500 of these tigers left in the wild are found in the Russian Far East.

Species: Warty Pig (Visayan)
Home: Chester Zoo
Conservation Status: Critically Endangered
These small pigs live on two of the Visayan Islands in the central Philippines. Boars (males) have three pairs of warts on their faces that may protect them from other boars' tusks during fights.

Species: Wombat (Common)
Home: Taronga Zoo
Conservation Status: Least Concern
The common wombat is a marsupial native to Australia. Wombats dig underground tunnel systems and eat grass and other plants. They breed every 2 years and produce a single baby, or joey, which remains in its mother's pouch for 5 months.